T0149313

MY FRIEND,

HENRY
MANCINI

Stories of Growing Up Together

John Weitzel with Lesley Himmel

WESTBOW
PRESS®
A DIVISION OF THOMAS NELSON
& ZONDERVAN

WestBow Press books may be ordered through booksellers or by contacting:

WestBow Press
A Division of Thomas Nelson & Zondervan
1663 Liberty Drive
Bloomington, IN 47403
www.westbowpress.com
1 (866) 928-1240

ISBN: 978-1-9736-5236-6 (hc)
ISBN: 978-1-5127-7628-7 (sc)
ISBN: 978-1-5127-7629-4 (e)

Library of Congress Control Number: 2017902631

Print information available on the last page.

WestBow Press rev. date: 01/29/2019

To Henry,

Thanks for being my huckleberry friend.
I cherish the many wonderful
times we spent together!
Until we meet again ...

Love, John

Henry Mancini (left) and
John Weitzel (right), 1966

To the memory of my son,
Lorman Bruce Weitzel,
1951–1973,
this book is affectionately dedicated.
May you be playing trumpet
in Henry Mancini's heavenly orchestra.

Many thanks to ...

John E. Weitzel Jr., Marketing Instructor
Western Michigan University
Kalamazoo, Michigan

Chris R. Hansen, Director of *Hark Up!*
Independent Arranger and Composer,
hansenchartsmusic.com
Grand Rapids, Michigan

Leah A. Kosanke
Grand Rapids, Michigan

Mia E. Larson, Illustrator
Belmont, Michigan

Contents

Foreword by Ginny Mancini

Henry Mancini, my late husband of forty-seven years, enjoyed worldwide success as a recording artist, concert performer, and film composer, for which he won a plethora of awards and accolades. He was respected by everyone with whom he worked and collaborated, and he developed lifelong friendships with many musicians worldwide.

What endeared him to me throughout our years together was his understanding of people and capacity for sound judgment apart from his intelligence, competence, or special talents. His insight, humor, and gentle strength were qualities that helped him handle situations and difficulties, including the horrific diagnosis of pancreatic cancer that ended his life.

To John Weitzel and his collaborator, Lesley Himmel, I extend my heartfelt thanks for sharing these delicious memories of Henry long before fortune smiled. I am truly grateful.

Sincerely,

Ginny Mancini

Preface by John Weitzel

*Y*ou may ask yourself, "How old is this man if he is writing a book about his friendship with Henry Mancini?" To answer this question, both Henry Mancini and I were born in 1924. So as I write this book in 2017, I am ninety-three years old—or, more correctly stated, ninety-three years young!

I was Henry Mancini's close friend through our school years and beyond. My family lived in Aliquippa, Pennsylvania, and Henry's family had moved from Cleveland, Ohio, to West Aliquippa. We lived about four miles from each other.

We met when we were twelve years old and in the seventh grade. We were both "only children," and we hit it off right from the start. We became friends and had fun just being together. I always called him Henry, but later in life, he went by Hank. He always called me Jack.

Henry was musically talented at a very young age. His father taught him to play the piccolo and the flute, and they played together in the local Italian band. I remember watching them stroll down the street playing all kinds of music. Henry also learned to play the piano. He would come to my house and entertain us by playing my mother's Chickering. He liked to perform!

As is well known, Henry Mancini grew up to become a very famous musician, songwriter, and orchestra director. He wrote wonderful songs, including "Moon River," "The Pink Panther," and so many more.

During the 1980s, my late wife, Dixie, and I received a beautiful letter and a large package of information from Henry Mancini praising our efforts to promote his music and his story (see photographs). Dixie and I would take our show on the road to local nursing homes, schools, and other interested organizations. Dixie was a professional piano player and a retired elementary school music teacher. I am a retired high school band director, and I accompanied her piano-playing on the organ. We produced live entertainment by playing Henry's famous music and telling his story. It was well-received by our audiences, and we enjoyed performing.

During this past year, I have befriended a fellow baritone player in the Grand Band of St. Cecilia Music Center in Grand Rapids, Michigan. Together, Lesley Himmel and I came up with an idea for once again sharing my memories of growing up with Henry Mancini. We are confident that, even after so many years, there is still a very large audience of Henry Mancini fans who will appreciate our new stories about this beloved man.

Preface by Lesley Himmel

$\mathcal{J}$t was quite by accident that I met John Weitzel. I was sitting in the baritone section of our Grand Band's weekly rehearsal at St. Cecilia Music Center when a group of Calder City Concert Band musicians came in to hear us play. They had been scheduled to play a concert next door at the First United Methodist Church, but it had just been cancelled.

Our excellent band director, Chris R. Hansen, invited them to "Get your horns out and join us!" And they did! John, being a baritone player, sat next to me, and I shared my music with him. He returned the next week and has been a member of the band ever since.

Chris selected a Henry Mancini number for us to play at our next concert. He learned that John had gone to school with Henry Mancini, and he wanted to hear his stories.

I offered to help John write down his memories. I was very excited to take on this new project. Soon, we had the twelve stories in this book.

It has been a pleasure to create this book with John. He is an amazing man. I know his readers will be in awe of his memories, just as I am.

1

Babes in Toyland

The year was 1936. Henry and I were both twelve years old and in the seventh grade at Aliquippa Junior High School in Aliquippa, Pennsylvania. We were both in the band. The drama teacher at our school asked our band director if she could recruit six students from our band to be wooden soldiers in her play, *Babes in Toyland*. Henry and I volunteered.

Rehearsals started after school. We were issued our soldier costumes. They were similar to band uniforms: red and black, with white crossed straps in front, and very tall stovepipe hats.

Henry could always make me laugh. It was contagious—you couldn't help yourself. He was just a very funny person. His timing was always perfect. He was a quiet person but always setting up the next prank.

Henry fit the profile of a tall wooden soldier perfectly. He was a very tall and slender boy. *Babes in Toyland* gave him many opportunities to play havoc with the whole scene. This is a glimpse of how rehearsals went.

The first trick by Henry was wearing his hat backward. It was hilarious! He would march out of step in our marching scenes on purpose, just to be funny. He made us all laugh.

Whenever there was a pivot-turning scene, he would deliberately pivot the opposite direction and run into people! It was all planned, of course. That was Henry.

When the actual show was performed, both of our mothers and fathers were in the audience. Luckily for everyone involved, Henry played it straight and did a wonderful job of being a wooden soldier.

2

Graffiti Artists

*T*he year was 1937. Henry and I were both thirteen years old and in the eighth grade, which was still part of our junior high school building. The big football game was that night. Our Aliquippa Indians were playing against Ambridge, our rival team. The whole school was excited for the night to begin.

Once a week, Henry and I would walk up a steep hill to our mechanical drawing class, which was located in the high school building. This was near the football field.

Henry got the bright idea that we should grab some chalk from the classroom and show our school pride. I was always a willing participant in anything Henry wanted to do. I thought he was great!

We stuffed our pockets full of chalk and headed outside after class. There was a cement corridor where the rival team would arrive and walk through the passageway. We took out our chalk and proceeded to write "Aliquippa Beat Ambridge!" all over the walls. It took a lot of work and a lot of time to get it just right. We wanted to do our part to intimidate the incoming rival team members as they were walking into our school territory.

Little did we know that our mechanical drawing teacher was watching us from the window above. His brother just happened to be the school principal. Unfortunately for Henry and me, he called the principal, who immediately hauled us into his office for a good reaming out. We were still junior high students, and now we were already in trouble at the high school.

We were instructed to get two buckets of soap and water and clean all that chalk off the cement walls. Ugh. It took an hour. But we did it, and were sufficiently chagrined to think twice about ever doing that again.

So much for helping school spirit!

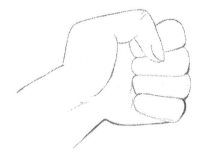

3

Bully in the Cafeteria

The year was 1938. Henry and I were both fourteen years old and in the ninth grade. As is the case in most schools everywhere, at any given time, there were bullies. Our school was no different.

My memory of a bully at Aliquippa Junior High School centered on our lunchroom cafeteria. All of my friends sat together every day at the same table for lunch, including Henry Mancini.

There was one mean kid at our table; I don't remember his name. His latest act of harassment to the rest of us was this: if anyone were to rest his hands on the top of the table (which is normal—we all do this without thinking about it), the mean kid would fist his hand into a hard ball and slam it down on the hand resting on the table. This would injure, at least temporarily, the recipient's hand. I know this sounds ridiculous, but for some reason, it was the prank at the time.

I felt the brunt of the hand slam once or twice myself. So did most of my friends at our table.

Henry, as we all know, needed his hands to play his instruments—the piccolo, flute, and piano. Incidentally, Henry had a fascination with being able to stretch the fingers on his left hand to reach a ten-key span on the piano. The jazz players of the day used the ten-key style for the left hand in most of their works. Henry had long fingers. I remember him sitting in school stretching his left thumb away from his fingers, pressing down on a desk, over and over. He finally did master the stretch for the ten-key chord.

At our cafeteria table, Henry was always very aware of what was going on around him. He would never absentmindedly relax his hands on the table.

However, one fine day, when Henry happened to be sitting next to the bully, he stretched his hand out on the table and watched out of the corner of his eye. When the bully made his move and attempted to slam his hand down on Henry's, Henry whipped his lightning-fast hand out of harm's way, causing the bully to slam his own hand down onto the very hard table. He let out a loud yelp, and all of the rest of us burst out laughing, including Henry.

Thanks to Mancini, that was the end of the bully in the cafeteria.

4

Streetlights and the Police

$\mathcal{T}$he year was 1939. Henry and I were both fifteen years old and in the tenth grade at Aliquippa High School. On this particular night, a group of select students, including Henry and me, attended a meeting at the Hi-Y club, which is a spin-off of the YMCA. We talked about good character and how to be good citizens in our community.

After the meeting was over, it just felt too early to go home. We were young, we had energy, and we just had to do something.

There were streetlights on every corner. The lights were atop very tall cement poles. There was the bulb, and there was a metal cover over the bulb. Well, it was every boy's goal to throw a stone, hit, and break the bulb. The sound of the smash was beautiful! All of my friends tried to break them, including me and Henry.

On this night, we were in a group of boys doing that very thing. (Keep in mind, we had just come from a meeting on how to be good citizens.) All of us were throwing stones at the light bulb, and someone hit it. *Crash!*

All of a sudden, pulling right up beside us was a police car. We heard the voice of an officer through his megaphone saying, "Okay, all of you boys stop right there and get into this car!"

Henry, being a little more street smart, disassociated himself from our group and just kept right on walking. He looked straight ahead and kept on walking right down the sidewalk. It was like he wasn't even with the rest of us. Henry always wore an old fedora hat, and he tilted his head just right so as not to make eye contact with the police. He blended right in with the other people on the sidewalk.

Once all of the rest of us were securely locked into the police car, the policeman pulled away and headed to the police station. We looked out our window to see Henry Mancini still walking down the sidewalk. He looked over at us, and with that wry "Mancini smile," he waved at us as we drove by.

None of the rest of us snitched on Henry. Friends wouldn't do that. It was, however, not pleasant to have our parents show up at the police station, listen to our sad story, and declare our consequences. We, of course, had to pay for the very expensive streetlight. My father was not happy about that!

Live and learn.

5

All-Star Band Festival

*T*he year was 1940. Henry and I were sixteen years old and juniors in high school. Each year, an All-Star Band Festival was held for chosen students in western Pennsylvania. Henry and I were both selected to play in this band, and I was the only student from our school selected to play a solo that year. The festival was held in the city of Punxsutawney.

If this city sounds familiar to you, there's a good reason. It is the place where the legendary groundhog Punxsutawney Phil comes out of his burrowed hole in the ground and, by seeing his shadow or not, determines whether we will have an early spring or another six weeks of winter.

At the festival, I played a trumpet solo. The music was an advanced and difficult piece, written by Harry James, called "Concerto for Trumpet."

And guess who accompanied *me* on the piano? Liberace! No, just kidding. It was Henry Mancini.

I played the solo, and Henry Mancini accompanied *me*, of all things! The accompaniment was much better than the solo.

The last note I had was a high C, and I missed it. Henry saw how upset I was and made a joke that Punxsutawney Phil heard me miss that note, and he came out of his hole with his ears covered and predicted six more weeks of winter.

6

The Joyride

The year was still 1940. Henry and I were both sixteen years old, and we were high-school juniors. I had just gotten my driver's license. My dad, in a questionable decision, allowed me to drive his 1937 Ford two-door sedan to school one day.

Three of my buddies, including Henry Mancini, encouraged me to skip afternoon classes and take them for a ride. Henry was seated in the front passenger seat, and my other two buddies were in the back seat. We decided to take Kane Road, a notorious "lovers' lane" in the Pennsylvania hills. The fact that it was snowing didn't deter us. And of course, in those days, there were no seat belts or safety features on the cars.

The boys encouraged me to see how fast I could make the car go. I got it up to fifty miles an hour! We were in the hills now, and to our right side was a very steep cliff. An unexpected curve in the road ahead led me to hit the brake. It put us into a spin on the gravel road. In that instant, all I could think of was that we were going to roll down that hill and crash.

There were no guardrails, but there was a culvert beside the road. Thankfully, it brought us to an abrupt stop. We were all pretty shook up, but basically unhurt. I can't say the same about the car! It incurred several scratches and a large dent. Fortunately, we were able to push it out of the ditch and get it back on the road. We headed back to school with our tails between our legs. That was the first and *last* time my dad allowed me to drive his car to school.

I often think that if the good Lord hadn't been with us on that day, it is possible that the world would have been deprived of the genius mind of Henry Mancini.

7

Music Theory Exam

The year was 1941. Henry and I were now seventeen years old and seniors in high school. Being close friends, we had always enjoyed many classes together, and especially being in the band. However, in our senior year, we were not assigned to any classes together.

Over the past couple of years, there had been some ongoing tension between Henry and our band director, possibly caused by the clashing of two strong and highly intelligent musical minds. Henry seemed frustrated by the strict rules and showed a bit of an attitude. It came to a head at the beginning of our senior year, and Henry was removed from band. However, later in the year, Henry was allowed back into the band, which I was very thankful for.

But at the start of the school year, we wanted to attend at least one class together. Henry encouraged me to take a music theory class with him, which I did.

The music theory teacher was a very strict disciplinarian. She wasn't about to put up with any nonsense from Henry Mancini. Even though Henry was disdainful of all the rules and regulations of formal music theory, we both managed to get to the end of the course without a major upheaval ... almost.

The final examination requirement was to follow all the rules of music theory and harmonize the song "America." I followed the rules, and I got an A. Henry made his own rules. When he turned in his paper to the teacher, she read it and abruptly tossed it into the wastebasket. Henry got an F!

As I think back on it, I sure wish I had been insightful enough to get into that wastebasket and retrieve that paper. I would have had a glimpse of the young genius mind of Henry Mancini.

8

Henry's Father

$\mathcal{H}$enry and I graduated from Aliquippa High School in 1941. When I left high school, I went to work for one year at the steel mill in Aliquippa so I could save money for college. Henry was able to go on a scholarship straight to the Juilliard School, a world-famous private conservatory of dance, drama, and music located in New York City.

The steel mill where I worked happened to also be the employer of Henry Mancini's father, Quinto Mancini. At the mill, I was a mail courier, and I was able to move around the whole plant delivering mail and messages to the various departments. On my regular route, I would pass Henry's father. Whenever he saw me, he would light up with excitement at the opportunity to tell me about Henry.

Quinto was a supervisor on an assembly line. He would literally stop all production on the line, making all the men stop and wait, while he told me about Henry's latest accomplishments. He was *so* proud of his son. Henry was setting the world on fire at Juilliard. They loved him, and he was rising to new heights at a young age.

I was, of course, always very happy to hear about Henry. However, I did feel guilty that his father was holding up the assembly line—which cost money! Because of this, I altered my route so as not to interrupt the work crew. From then on, our communication was by telephone. I also occasionally stopped by Henry's house to chat with Quinto and Anna, Henry's mother. They welcomed me warmly.

I feel that Henry Mancini's father, Quinto, should be given recognition for his influence and sacrifice in enabling the success of his son. During those Depression years, money was scarce, but Henry's father somehow provided him with flute and piano lessons. In Henry's teen years, his father would drive him to Pittsburgh for private lessons with music teacher Max Adkins, studying music arranging and directing. By age seventeen, Henry's early talents and accomplishments opened the door for his training at Juilliard. A young genius was on his way to becoming a star.

9

Not Yet Famous

After graduating from high school in 1941, Henry went straight to the Juilliard School in New York City. Toward the end of his first year at Juilliard, he turned eighteen and registered for the draft.

Henry and I served in the military at the same time. We stayed in contact during those years by letter. I was assigned to the Army Air Corps communications in Texas. Henry was assigned to the Army Air Corps and did his basic training in Atlantic City. The famous big band director, Glenn Miller, was a captain in the Army, also stationed in Atlantic City. Following a chance meeting between the two, Glenn Miller was so impressed by Henry's musical skills that he personally recommended that Henry be reassigned to an Air Force band, to Henry's great relief! Henry had a varied experience, including playing a pump organ for a company chaplain in the war fields.

I was assigned to Scott Field in Illinois in 1944. I knew Henry was stationed there at that time, and I tried to make contact—but I found out that he and his band had just shipped out for overseas. I missed seeing him by one day.

By 1946, Henry and I had both completed our stints in the military. Henry went back to New York, but he did not return to Juilliard. He was hired as a pianist for the Tex Beneke Band (which replaced the old Glenn Miller Band, as Glenn Miller was missing in action during the war). While on the road with the Tex Beneke Band, Henry met Virginia "Ginny" O'Connor, a beautiful and talented singer for the band.

Early in 1947, Henry was scheduled to play a show in Cleveland. My fiancée, Dixie, and I met him at a drugstore for an hour before the concert. We had burgers and Cokes. Henry seemed just the same as he always had. He wore his old fedora hat and raincoat. I'm sure it was the same hat and coat he wore all through high school. With great excitement, he told us about his fiancée, Ginny.

I naively showed Henry a new piece of music that Dixie and I had written, "The Gum Shoe Hop," and asked if he could help us get it published. We had also written the College of Wooster, Ohio, fight song, "Hail to the Black and Gold," which is still used to this day. Ironically, Henry said he was still having trouble getting his own work published. His name wasn't known yet. We went to see him perform that night in the Tex Beneke Band. He was an excellent musician, but not yet famous.

Early that summer, at our home in Aliquippa, we heard a rattly old car coming down Fillmore Street. It was Henry! He was bubbling over with all kinds of news. He had quit the band and was moving to Hollywood, California, to marry Ginny and write for the movies. During the coming years, Henry and Ginny had a son, Chris, and twin daughters, Monica and Felice. Henry worked for Universal Studios and, indeed, became *very* famous!

10

Guest Conductor

The year was 1966. It had been twenty-five years since Henry Mancini, my childhood friend since seventh grade, and I graduated from high school together. We were both forty-two years old now. We had gone our separate ways. I was a high school band director in Alliance, Ohio, and Henry was a legendary composer/arranger living in Hollywood, California. We did, however, keep in touch during all those years.

As my annual spring concert at Alliance High School approached, I suggested that we bring in Henry Mancini to join me as the guest conductor. At this time in his career, Henry was internationally famous and had earned numerous Oscars, Grammys, and various other awards. I was reluctant to ask him, lest he be too busy with his work to comply with my request. But I did write a letter. And to my pleasure, Henry accepted my invitation to appear at my spring concert in Alliance.

My public relations friend let the entire town know that Henry Mancini was coming. The townspeople were thrilled, and every ticket was sold. The members of my band were ecstatic in anticipation.

The day finally came—April 16, which was also Henry's forty-second birthday! I started the concert with a couple of opening numbers, and then Henry came onstage. He was met with great enthusiasm from the audience. He conducted "The Pink Panther," *Peter Gunn* music, "Moon River," and several of his other great pieces.

I always ended my concerts with "The Stars and Stripes Forever." Before each concert, it was determined which student would get the honor of playing the piccolo part in the trio. For this concert, my student, Bob, was chosen. He was a seventeen-year-old boy in the twelfth grade.

I conducted the march. When we got to the trio, Bob stood up to play his piccolo part. There was a stirring in the audience, and I looked around. Henry had come onto the stage with *his* piccolo! He stood next to Bob, and they played the piccolo part together. Bob's eyes were huge with amazement, but he played it through to the end. The audience stood up and cheered. I am sure that Bob will never forget that moment— and neither will I!

Following the concert, my family and a group of colleagues and band boosters attended a reception to celebrate Henry's visit and his birthday. We presented him with a very large cake—a replica of a grand piano. I have a treasured memory of Henry cutting the cake and handing me the first piece. It was a memorable evening.

I was pleased that Henry stayed through the weekend, giving us a chance to reminisce. There were many times to follow over the years when Henry and I were able to be together and share great memories. We both cherished our lifelong friendship.

11

My Son, Bruce

I married my wife, Annelu "Dixie" Hutson, in 1947, while we were students at the College of Wooster, Ohio. Our firstborn son, Lorman Bruce Weitzel, came along in 1951. We were also blessed with a second son, John Ellis Weitzel, born in 1953. John is now a marketing instructor at Western Michigan University and resides with his wife, Katie, in Kalamazoo, Michigan. As parents, we couldn't have had more pride or love for our children. But this story is just about Bruce.

My son, Bruce, was a wonderful child—energetic, handsome, smart, playful, and a great student all through school. I gave Bruce my trumpet while he was in the fourth grade, and I taught him to play. He had a natural talent for music, and he became a very excellent trumpet player.

While a young boy, Bruce started showing signs of illness. When he was in the ninth grade, we took him to the Cleveland Clinic and were given the news that he had Crohn's disease. It was similar to cancer, in that it would go into remission, often for long periods of time. Bruce was a brave child, though, and just went on with school and life as usual.

In band, Bruce was first-chair trumpet player all through school. He always earned first place ribbons and trophies for trumpet solos in competitions. Bruce graduated from high school in 1969.

He attended Kent State University in Ohio, where he studied trumpet performance, music composition, and directing. He was following a path much like that of Henry Mancini. Bruce played trumpet for the Kent State Big Band-Jazz Band, and he was the star player! Bruce married his hometown girlfriend, Sandy, and they moved to Hollywood, California, in 1971.

By this time, Bruce was very talented and took a job working with Doc Severinsen, a famous trumpet player who led the NBC Orchestra on *The Tonight Show* featuring Johnny Carson. Bruce was also employed as a music writer for John Elizalde, music supervisor at Cannon Studios, who did the music for the TV detective show *Cannon*.

During this same time period, Bruce signed a contract to play trumpet in a recording session with the Henry Mancini Orchestra. They were going to do background music for a movie. This was another testament to my friendship with Henry and the influence and loyalty he had for my family.

But fate can be cruel. The very day before Bruce was to play with Henry Mancini, he became very sick and went into the hospital. This bad upheaval of his illness was to be his last. Sadly, Bruce passed away in the hospital March 28, 1973, at the very young age of twenty-one. I have no words to describe that day.

We received condolences from Henry Mancini and John Elizalde. Ironically, we received a paycheck for the recording session that Bruce would have worked for Henry. The musicians' union required it. Once you sign a contract, you are paid, no matter what. So Bruce received one check from Henry Mancini's organization.

Everyone felt the loss of a budding young musician and writer. One can only speculate on what Bruce would have accomplished if he had been allowed to live a full life. We can only hold to our faith in God that we will all be together again in heaven someday. Bruce will forever be missed.

12

Blossom Center

$\mathcal{T}$he year was 1975. Henry and I were both fifty-one years old.

Blossom Center is a huge venue for summer outdoor concerts near Cleveland, Ohio. It is the summer home of the Cleveland Orchestra. The pavilion and hillside lawn fill to twenty thousand patrons. It is in the Akron-Canton area, south of Cleveland.

Henry Mancini would perform there once every year, conducting the Cleveland Orchestra. There was always one guest star. For the concert in the summer of '75, the guest was James Galway, the world-famous flutist. Henry and James played a flute duet during this concert.

My family and I were in the audience that evening. Through prior communication, Henry knew we would be there.

In the middle of this concert, Henry stopped the show. He said, "I have a very important old friend here tonight!" He called out my name, "John Weitzel!" and he told me to "Stand up, John!" He then proceeded to tell the audience of twenty thousand people that he had known me since seventh grade, and we had been the best of friends all through school and ever since then.

He took the time to tell everyone I was the band director at Alliance High School, about thirty miles south of there. He praised all the accomplishments I was making with my band and the national trips we had taken. His words took my breath away. I felt like I was on cloud nine!

After the concert, we were escorted into the greenroom backstage, where Henry and I gave each other a big hug. It was great to be with my old friend again. While backstage, Henry turned and said, "John, I would like you to meet James Galway." So as an extra bonus, I got to shake the hand of this famous flute player.

The evening was wonderful. It was a huge honor for me to be recognized in such a big way by Henry Mancini. It reinforced the affection we held for each other as lifelong friends.

Conclusion

Sadly, Henry Mancini lived to be only seventy years old. He was born on April 16, 1924, in Cleveland, Ohio. He passed away on June 14, 1994, in Los Angeles, California, of pancreatic cancer.

I often wonder about all the music that the world has been deprived of because Henry was no longer here to write it. However, I have no doubt that Henry has been an inspiration to countless musicians, composers, and directors who have produced new works because of their contact with the genius mind of Henry Mancini.

My childhood friend had an amazing life. I couldn't be happier for him. I am very thankful for the lifelong friendship we shared.

Until we meet again, Henry ...

Love, John

Photographs

HENRY MANCINI
Aliquippa High School Senior Picture 1941

Class Prophesy:
MANCINI--"Hen", a true music lover, collects records, plays in the band, and has even composed several beautiful selections. He wishes to continue his study of music and to have an orchestra of his own someday.

JOHN WEITZEL
Aliquippa High School Senior Picture 1941

Class Prophesy:
WEITZEL--"Jack", well-known president of the band and president of his home room, has given many trumpet solos in assemblies and has worked diligently for the betterment of the Hi-Y and the orchestra. Enjoying music as he does, he plans to further this study after graduation.

Aliquippa High School Band 1941
Under the Direction of Dr. Davenport
(Henry in oval on left, John in oval on right)

HENRY MANCINI
9229 SUNSET BOULEVARD
LOS ANGELES, CALIFORNIA 90069
(213) 278-4104

December 14, 1983

Ms. Dixie Weitzel
1560 Overlook Drive
Alliance, Ohio 44601

Dear Dixie:

I was very pleased that you are thinking about
presenting some of my music in one of your
programs.

Enclosed is a copy of my press kit with pictures.
Also find a Song Book and a copy of the latest
themes that are available. I hope that this
material will be of some hope to you.

From the sound of your letter you and Jack are
doing quite well. Our whole clan is engaged in
one thing or another. Our grandson, Chris, is
seven and is living with us, and he is a constant
source of recycled joy.

Have a happy Christmas!

Love,

Hank

Letter from Henry Mancini, 1983

JOHN WEITZEL   HENRY MANCINI
. . . Schoolmates Reunited . . .

2 Aliquippans To Perform Together

ALLIANCE, Ohio — T w o 1942 graduates of Aliquippa, High School, who carved separate but successful musical careers for themselves, will be together on the same stage twice this Saturday.

Composer Henry Mancini will be the guest artist and conductor when the Alliance High School Band presents its spring concert.

The nationally known band is directed by J o h n Weitzel.

The men were high school chums, and Weitzel invited Mancini to be the featured attraction this year with a l l proceeds going toward t h e band's uniform fund.

Mancini will be spotlighted in a segment of the matinee and evening performances and then will direct the band during the second half of the concert which will feature all Mancini numbers.

The Alliance High S c h o o l Choir will sing two Mancini originals.

Mancini is making the trip from his Los Angeles home for expenses only.

WEITZEL has literally put the band, high school and community on the map by taking his band before millions of TV viewers and spectators at professional football games each season since 1962.

The band has appeared in Michigan, New York, Pennsylvania as well as throughout Ohio.

In addition, the bandsmen marched as the only Buckeye State Band in the 1964, N e w Year's Eve Orange Bowl Parade in Miami, Fla.

Weitzel has been at the helm here since 1961.

Mancini's appearance here will fall on his 42nd birthday. The Alliance High School Band Boosters Club will hold a private reception for him following the evening concert.

Newspaper Article, 1966

67

The Famed

Henry Mancini
with

The Alliance High School Band

SAT., APRIL 16
2:15 - 8 P.M.

ALLIANCE HIGH SCHOOL
AUDITORIUM

SUPPORT HIGH SCHOOL BOND ISSUE MAY 3

Henry Mancini, Guest Conductor
Spring Concert Program, 1966

John (left) and Henry (right), Spring Concert, 1966

Cake presented to Henry for his
forty-second birthday
at concert reception, 1966

Henry (left), Dixie (center), and John (right), 1966

Bruce, 1970

John Jr. (left) and Bruce (right), 1965

Autographed photo of Henry Mancini
presented to Bruce and John Jr., 1966

About the Authors

*J*ohn Ellis Weitzel has lived a very active life. Raised by parents Lorman Bruce and Helene Janet Weitzel in Aliquippa, Pennsylvania, he grew up loving music and took trumpet lessons at an early age. Following high school, he served in the US Army during WWII.

John and his wife, Dixie, earned bachelor's degrees in music from the College of Wooster, Ohio, and John earned a master's in music education from Columbia University in New York City. They raised two sons, Bruce and John Jr.

John worked for thirty-five years as a high school band director in East Liverpool and Alliance, Ohio, winning many awards and leading his band in front of millions of TV viewers and spectators at professional football games. He is now retired and currently resides in Grand Rapids, Michigan. At age ninety-three, he remains very active—spending time with his family and friends, playing baritone horn in several bands, and telling stories of his friendship with Henry Mancini to retirement and nursing home residents and other interested groups in the area.

Coauthor Lesley Elizabeth Himmel enjoyed growing up on a farm near Brown City, Michigan, with parents Nick and Alma Himmel, and siblings Susan, Beverly, Debra, and Nick. Following high school, she earned a bachelor's degree and graduate certificate in business education from Central Michigan University and worked in the field of education. Lesley is now retired and lives in Grand Rapids, Michigan. She enjoys time with daughters Emily (Cory) and Leah (Zachary), and grandchildren Mia, Nolan, Vaughn, Brooke, and Dean, also attending church and playing in a community band.

Printed in the United States
By Bookmasters